THE OLD TIMER SAYS

Published by the Wisconsin Historical Society Press
Publishers since 1855

The Wisconsin Historical Society helps people connect to the past by collecting, preserving, and sharing stories. Founded in 1846, the Society is one of the nation's finest historical institutions.
Join the Wisconsin Historical Society: wisconsinhistory.org/membership

Printed in Canada
Cover design by TG Design
Interior design and layout by Mayfly Design
Front cover illustration © 2020 by John Zimm

24 23 22 21 20 1 2 3 4 5

♾ The paper used in this publication meets the minimum requirements of the American National Standard for Information Sciences—Permanence of Paper for Printed Library Materials, ANSI Z39.48-1992.

"When we forget our histories, we forget who we are." I first heard these words many years ago from my father, a life-long farmer. He often reminded me of how lessons from his past influenced what he did on the farm. I've never forgotten those words, and I've lived by them ever since.

I began writing in a journal when I was twelve. I was recovering from polio and had been confined to bed for several weeks. My Aunt Louise often stopped by with a new book for me to read, but one day she brought with her a small diary. "I thought you might want to jot down each day's happenings," she told me. I still have that diary (and all the journals I've kept since—I am currently writing in volume forty-four).

Writing down daily happenings, thoughts, and feelings in a journal like this one is an important way to capture your personal history. Even if you have never written in a journal, it's not too late to start. Journal writing is for everyone, not only for "writers." It doesn't matter how much you write or what you write, only *that you write.*

A journal is a personal thing, and there is no "right way" to keep one. You might dash off only a few words here and there, or you might find yourself writing long pages of detailed, flowing narrative. Your entries might consist of a brief recounting of each day's activities, or they might include lists of plants and animals you've seen or places you'd like to visit. Your journal could be a place to write down your future goals, recipes you'd like to cook, favorite song lyrics, notes about your dreams, comments about a book you're reading, or short stories starring your own made-up characters. You might even include sketches or photographs or other visual tidbits.

My journal entries always begin with the date, the temperature, and a few additional notes about the weather. (It's the old farmer in me.) Then I write about something that happened that day. It might be about family; I'm writing a lot about my grandkids these days. Or it might be about something that is happening at my farm, such as a new bird species I've spotted, a wildflower that has sprouted in my prairie, or the progress of my vegetable garden. I sometimes include a news story about a friend—I'll paste it right onto a page. If my wife and I see a play or a movie, I might include the ticket. When I make a major purchase, like a new car or tractor, I record the model, make, and price. (What fun it is to compare the cost of a new car in 2020 with one purchased in 1960!)

Besides recording our personal history, writing in a journal can help us clarify our thoughts, feelings, and observations. When I have a problem or don't understand something, I begin writing about it, and what has been murky often begins to become clear. The process of writing about a challenge often leads to a solution. Journal writing also forces me to consider what is truly important in my life. I don't have time to record everything—none of us does. What I have chosen to write about usually turns out to be what was most important to me at the time.

Every year on about January 1, I write about the happenings in the previous year that I feel were most important to me and to my family—anything from a health challenge to applauding a grandchild's graduation from high school or college. Then I write down my goals for the year ahead. They might be related to my writing career or to things I want to do on our farm, or they might be goals or reminders of a more personal nature. Here's an example from a few years ago:

Some things to do in the New Year:

Take time to see the whiteness of fresh-fallen snow.

Watch the sun set when the temperature is below freezing and the sky is steel blue.

Listen for the silence of winter, when snow buries the land and the cold tightens its grip.

Sit by a fireplace and do nothing expect listen to the pop of the fire and smell the hint of wood smoke that sneaks into the room.

Remember that doing nothing is sometimes the most important thing you can do.

Journal writing also helps me tap into my subconscious. One thought or memory seems to trigger another, bringing to the surface recollections of long-ago people and events that I didn't even realize I remembered. I have taught writing for many years, and I've seen this happen for many of my students as well. By responding to a few simple memory triggers or prompts, they're often surprised to find what they have tucked away below the surface.

On these journal pages, I've provided some prompts that I hope will trigger a memory or inspire your own creativity. Many of these "Old Timer" sayings are things I heard growing up on a farm in central Wisconsin in the 1930s and 1940s. In those days, farmers shared a good deal of the work, especially at harvest time, when they went from farm to farm to help with the grain threshing, silo filling, and corn husking. After the labor was finished, the neighbors gathered to share not only a meal but jokes, tall tales, and recollections, many taking the form of one-liners.

Some of those sayings contained powerful wisdom, and

some had multiple meanings. "There's less mud at the top of the hill" is literally true, but it's also an encouragement to folks to avoid wallowing in confusion or gossip—to rise above. Many Old Timer sayings captured what life was like during the Great Depression. I'll never forget what one neighborhood Old Timer said when I asked him how he was doing: "I was born with nothing, and I have most of it left." And some of the Old Timer sayings seemed to make no sense at all, yet they were often repeated. My mother, a full-blooded German, would often say, "We Germans must stick together; everybody for himself."

My first job after college was as a county extension agent in the 1950s, working with farm families. Many of the men and women I met with would drop bits of country wisdom during our conversations, some conveying deep meaning, others just for fun. More than once I heard, "No matter what direction a north wind comes from, it always blows cold," usually said with a big smile. Or this from a person commenting on skimpy bathing wear: "If God meant for you to run around naked, you would have been born that way." Of course, the weather was a frequent star of these farmers' commentary, as in this description of northern winters: "The winters used to be so cold that when a man cussed, the words froze, and you didn't hear them until the following spring."

I've selected Old Timer sayings for this book that I hope will make you smile, make you remember, and make you want to write something of your own. Here is one of my favorites: "A fellow was a man of few words. When he spoke, folks felt even fewer words would have been better."

Here is a place for your words, be they few or many.

When we forget our histories,
we forget who we are.

You are never too old to learn something new.

Never underestimate the wisdom of a cow.

Most of what absolutely must be done today
can wait until tomorrow.

A good night's sleep can do much
to calm an angry mind.

In our never-ending quest for more, we sometimes forget to appreciate what we already have.

Nothing speaks louder of your hope
for the future than planting a tree.

A good hen doesn't cackle until she's laid an egg.

Wisdom is not a gift, it must be earned.

Often the most difficult thing to do
is come out from behind yourself.

In your busy life, take time to remember.

If you are doing nothing,
how do you know when you are finished?

Sometimes the hardest part of learning something new is getting rid of an old idea.

The fish bite the best when the wind is in the west.

There is a time to hurry and a time to slow down, a time for thinking and a time for doing, a time to hear and a time to be heard, a time to speak and a time to listen.

Four-letter words to think about:

Give. Feel. Sing. Look. Hear. Love. Hope. Play.

There is great beauty in silence.

Nothing cripples more than fear.

Sometimes it's important to just breathe deeply.

Waiting for opportunity to knock on your door is like waiting for a train after the tracks have been torn up and the depot is closed.

No one can steal a memory.

Wherever you go, that's where you are.

It is okay to not know everything
and wise to admit it.

Why do we praise light and fear darkness?

Most of us find happiness
when we aren't looking for it.

Nobody is making more land. What we've got is what we've got, so we had better take care of it.

To learn about what's up ahead,
talk to people on their way back.

Do nothing in haste, except
running away from an angry dog.

Plant one kernel of sweet corn for the table,
one for a crow, and one for dry weather.

Find joy in simple things.

Just because you have a lot of education
doesn't mean you know anything.

Don't forget the importance of a good example.

Getting into something is usually easier
than getting out of it.

Sometimes it takes a while to realize
that we can't know everything.

Watch the new moon. If it's tipped so you can't hang a pail of water on its tip, rain is on the way.

Words not spoken can be
the most important things we have to say.

When you whack a hornet's nest, expect to be stung.

It's time to plant your corn in spring when
new oak leaves are the size of a squirrel's ear.

Search for humor when nothing seems funny.

In any journey, it's important to stop from time to time and be thankful for the distance you've traveled.

Know your history, but don't get stuck there.

You can count the number of seeds in an apple, but the number of apples in a seed is impossible to know.

We are all teachers; we are all learners.

Tall trees don't always provide the most shade.

It is an unfortunate person who does not have wood to split, a garden to hoe, or a trail to hike.

How you swing the ax isn't as important
as where the ax blade strikes the tree.

If you put all your eggs in one basket,
be sure to keep your eye on the basket.

Our lives are a series of little stories that add up to the big story of who we are, what we believe, and what we value.

There are no shortcuts to important places.

Books do not scold when you blunder, laugh when you are ignorant, or hide when you seek them.

A garden is one kind of miracle.

A rainy day is nature's way of interrupting the headlong rush that seems to be the fate of most of us.

Patience is something you just can't have too much of.

It's all right to have nothing to say
as long as you don't say it.

Worry is like being stuck in deep mud.
The wheels keep turning but nothing happens.

Do the best you can with what you've got.

Some bridges should be crossed
before you get to them.

When you go out on a limb,
make sure that no one with a saw is in sight.

There are those who have nothing to do
but do it exceedingly well.

When it's over, it's not over, except when it is.

Avoid sticking your hand in a dark hole.

Happiness for a farmer is a barn roof that doesn't leak,
a pasture fence that doesn't need fixing,
and a daylong rain in May.

Slow down.

It's hard to get from here to there if you're unclear about here and haven't thought much about there.

A gimpy leg does not mean a gimpy mind.

Ever listen to someone who talked on and on
hoping to come up with something to say?

The greatest reward for a job well done
is having done it.

An old horse, an old dog, and an old farmer
have much in common: they are slow but wise.

The brightest light can come from darkness.

The grass may be greener on the other side of the fence, but it doesn't matter if you can't crawl over.

Sometimes doing nothing
is the most important thing you can do.

When you are eating an apple and find a worm,
be thankful it isn't half a worm.

There is no need to fear the wind
if your haystack is tied down.

You don't learn patience by hurrying.

Sometimes the harder you look, the less you see.

Try, try again, and maybe try once more.
But then try something different.

Listen for the quiet;
you'll be astounded at what you hear.

There is more to planting corn
than putting seed in the ground.

What you know is something
nobody can take away from you.

In a willing team of horses, one is willing to pull and the other is willing to let him.

It's better to make your own dust
than to travel in someone else's.

Sometimes the hardest thing to do is to keep doing.

If bigger is better, why is a dime worth more than a nickel?

First things first, but not necessarily in that order.

When you think you've done the best you can,
consider that a starting point for making it even better.

When something goes wrong, write about it.
You'll feel better.

The road home is often the longest.

The land not only feeds our bodies
but nourishes our souls.

No matter how fast things change,
hold on to a few that don't.

Sometimes the best thing to do is to go fishing.

Some of the best of what is next has been here all along.

Next year will be better.

It's never too late to tell your story.

Jerry Apps is a former county extension agent and professor emeritus for the College of Agriculture and Life Sciences at the University of Wisconsin–Madison. Today he works as a rural historian, full-time writer, and creative writing instructor. Jerry is the author of more than forty books on topics ranging from barns, one-room schools, cranberries, and cheese factories to the Ringlingville Brothers Circus and the Civilian Conservation Corps. He has kept a journal since he was twelve.